Space Vehicles

Patricia Walsh

Illustrations by Mark Adamic

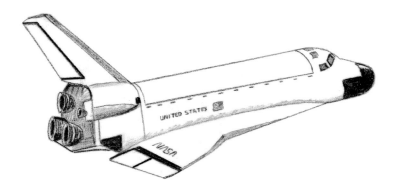

Heinemann Library
Chicago, Illinois

© 2001, 2006 Heinemann Library
a division of Reed Elsevier Inc.
Chicago, Illinois

Customer Service 888-454-2279
Visit our website at www.heinemannraintree.com

Designed by Kimberly R. Miracle and Q2A Creative
Illustrated by Mark Adamic
Photos by Kim Saar, p. 4; Mark Ferry, p. 5
Printed in China by WKT

10 09 08 07 06
10 9 8 7 6 5 4 3 2 1

New edition ISBNs: 1-4034-8924-6 (hardcover)
                    1-4034-8931-9 (paperback)

The Library of Congress has cataloged the first edition as follows:
Walsh, Patricia, 1951-
       Space Vehicles / by Patricia Walsh ; illustrations by Mark Adamic.
          p. cm. – (Draw It!)
       Includes bibliographical references and index.
Summary: Presents instructions for drawing various spacecraft and
vehicles, real and imaginary.
ISBN 1-57572-350-6 (lib. bdg.)
1. Space vehicles in art – Juvenile literature. 2. Drawing – Technique – Juvenile literature.
[1. Space vehicles in art. 2. Drawing – Technique.] I. Adamic, Mark, 1962-ill. II. Title.

NC825.S58 W35 2001
743'.896294– dc21

                                                    00025405

Acknowledgments
Cover photograph reproduced with permission of Royalty-Free/Getty.

Every effort has been made to contact copyright holders of any material reproduced in this book. Any omissions will be rectified in subsequent printings if notice is given to the publisher.

Disclaimer
All the Internet addresses (URLs) given in this book were valid at the time of going to press. However, due to the dynamic nature of the Internet, some addresses may have changed, or sites may have changed or ceased to exist since publication. While the author and publisher regret any inconvenience this may cause readers, no responsibility for any such changes can be accepted by either the author or the publisher.

Some words are shown in bold, **like this**. You can find out what they mean by looking in the glossary.

Contents

Introduction

Would you like to improve the pictures that you draw? Well, you can! In this book, the artist has drawn pictures of space vehicles. He has used lines and shapes to draw each picture in small, simple steps. Follow these steps and your picture will come together.

Here is advice from the artist:

- Always draw lightly at first.
- Draw all the shapes and pieces in the right places.
- Pay attention to the spaces between the lines as well as the lines themselves.
- Add details and **shading** to finish your drawing.
- And finally, erase the lines you don't need.

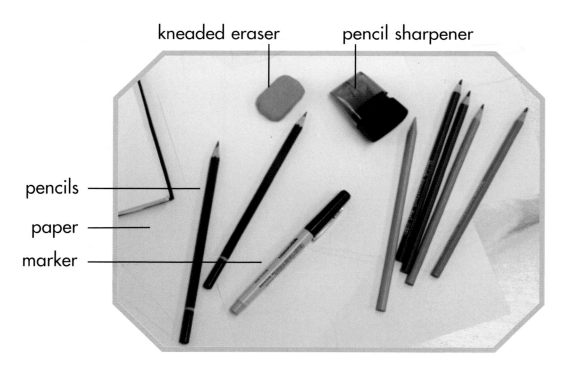

You only need a few supplies to get started.

There are just a few things you need for drawing:

- a pencil (medium or soft). You might also use a fine marker or pen to finish your drawing.

- a pencil sharpener

- paper

- an eraser. A **kneaded eraser** works best. It can be squeezed into small or odd shapes. This eraser can also make pencil lines lighter without erasing them.

Now are you ready? Do you have everything? Then turn the page and let's draw!

The drawings in this book were done by Mark Adamic. Mark started out by **doodling** in elementary school. In college, he studied art and history. Now he works full time as an illustrator, but his hobby is drawing airplanes. Mark's favorite plane is the P-51 Mustang. His advice to anyone who wants to become an artist is, "Don't just draw your favorite thing. Draw everything, because that's the way you learn. Draw every day, and study other artists."

X-15 Rocket Plane

In the 1960s, X-15 **test pilots** flew to the edge of the Earth's **atmosphere**. The X-15s flew at supersonic speeds. These test flights provided new information about spacecraft and the atmosphere.

Step 1:
Draw a long oval shape like an ice-cream stick. Make one end pointed for the nose.

Step 2:
Add a bump to the top of the pointed end for the pilot's **canopy**. Add one wing and one **tailplane**. Make their shapes short and narrow to show that they are pointed toward you.

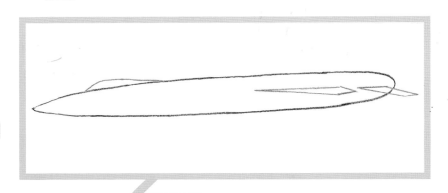

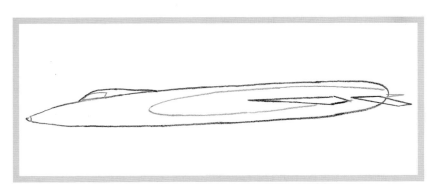

Step 3:
Draw a short line across the tip of the nose. Draw a small rectangle on the bump for a **cockpit** window. Draw a long oval on the side for the rocket engine. Add a short, straight line to the tailplane.

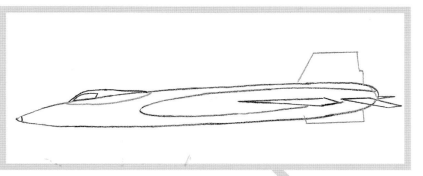

Step 4:

Draw a curved line under the cockpit window. At the round end, draw a rectangular shape above the body and a smaller rectangular shape below for the fins.

Step 5:

Draw a small rectangle, a larger triangle shape, and a tiny triangle along the side. Add a tiny triangle behind the canopy. Add **horizontal** lines and a small, backward F shape to the large rear fin.

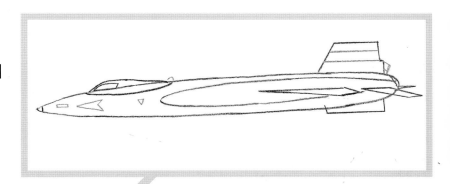

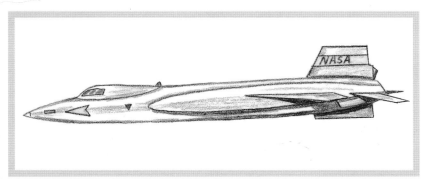

Step 6:

Write **NASA** between two **parallel** lines on the upper fin. **Shade** the plane and the cockpit window. Darken the areas underneath the body of the plane.

Mercury Capsule

The first manned spacecraft of the United States was the tiny Mercury **capsule**. In 1961, **astronaut** Alan Shepard made the first U.S. manned space flight. In 1962, John Glenn became the first American to **orbit** Earth.

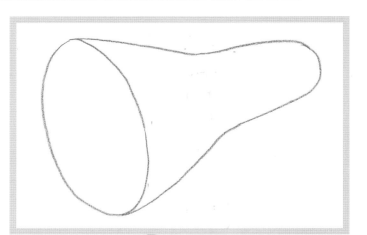

Step 1:

Draw a bell shape. Draw a large oval at the end of the bell to make the **heat shield**.

Step 2:

Draw a circle near the center of the heat shield. Draw two curved lines across the handle of the bell shape to divide the capsule into three sections.

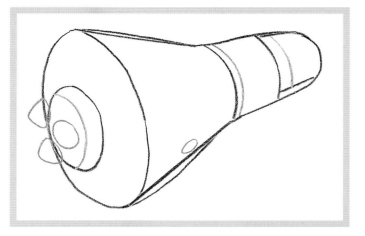

Step 3:

Add three small cone shapes and a curved line to the circle on the heat shield. The cones are **retrorockets**. Draw a small circle on the large section for the astronaut's window. Add two curved lines to the handle of the bell shape.

Step 4:

Add half a square around the tiny window. Draw three small ovals between the retrorocket cones. Make a little C shape on the top of each retrorocket.

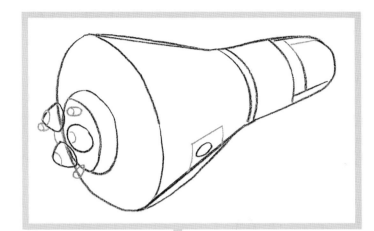

Step 5:

Draw two pairs of double lines on the heat shield. Add a straight line to the large section, five **parallel** lines to the middle section, and a line and a circle to the end section.

Step 6:

Draw several straight lines the length of the large section. Then add a lot of short lines in the spaces between the longer lines. Add soft **shading** and darken the important lines.

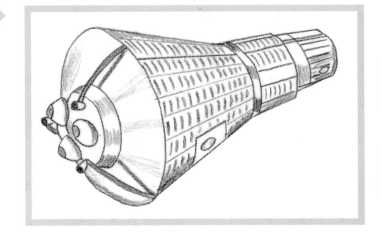

Saturn 5 Rocket
and Launch Tower

It took the powerful Saturn 5 rocket to boost **astronauts** to the moon in 1968. The first two **stages** carried fuel to launch the rocket. The third stage provided the power to put the Apollo spacecraft into moon **orbit**.

Step 1:

Draw a tall box that is wider at its base to make the launch tower. Draw a very short box next to the base for the launch pad. Draw a thin tube with a thicker one next to it just below the base of the launch pad. Draw a tall tube on top of the launch pad for the rocket.

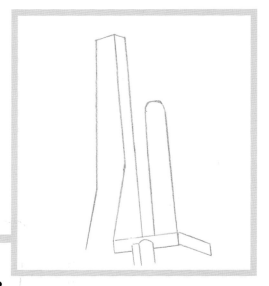

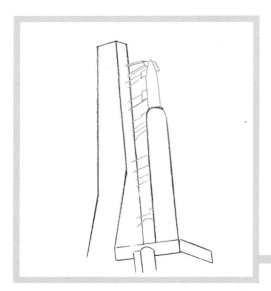

Step 2:

Draw a bullet shape on top of the rocket. This is the third stage of the rocket. Add nine pairs of short straight lines between the launch tower and the rocket.

Step 3:

Draw three triangular shapes at the base of the rocket. Draw a needle point on top. Add curved lines and rectangles to the side of the rocket.

Step 4:

Add a thin triangle to the top of the launch tower. Draw a line down the side of the tower. Make straight lines across the tower to divide it into many sections. Then add short **vertical** lines to the sides of the launch pad.

Step 5:

Draw a **diagonal** line through each section of the launch tower. Use short lines to fill in the spaces between the line pairs that connect the tower and the rocket.

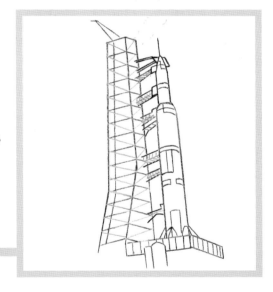

Step 6:

Darken some of the rectangular markings on the rocket. Add **shading** to the rocket and the launch pad.

Lunar Rover

The **Lunar** Rover was a lightweight electric car. Apollo **astronauts** first used it on the moon in 1971. The rover helped them explore the surface and collect moon rocks.

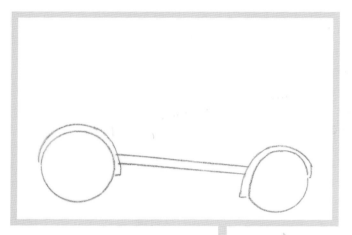

Step 1:

Start with two circles for the wheels. Connect them with two straight lines to make the rover's frame. Draw curved lines over the wheels to make **fenders**.

Step 2:

Draw three circles, one inside the other, on the wheels. Add a triangle near the middle of the frame. Draw a seat above the triangle. The seat, steering box, and batteries are different-sized rectangles along the frame.

Step 3:

Add **crosshatching** to the seat back. Use tall rectangles to draw racks for equipment, tools, and sample bags behind the seat. Above the front wheels, draw a dish-shaped antenna on a pole.

Step 4:

Near the center in front of the seat, use rectangular shapes and straight lines to draw the navigation system and controls. Draw two parts of a circle for the far front wheel.

Step 5:

Add straight line details to the wheels and the frame. Draw a half circle next to the seat and two levers on top of it.

Step 6:

Draw a Z-shaped line from the antenna to a camera. Draw short lines around the rims of the wheels. Add **shading** to the seat back and wheels.

Space Shuttle

The first Space Transportation System, or space shuttle, was launched in 1981. This reusable spacecraft has made many trips to space. **Astronauts** on board launch, bring back, and repair satellites. They also perform scientific experiments.

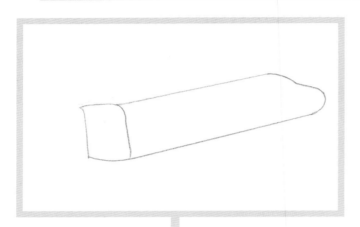

Step 1:

Draw a rectangle for the body of the shuttle, but make one end rounded and narrower than the rest of the rectangle. Draw a square at the other end.

Step 2:

Draw a triangular wing along the side. Only one wing can be seen in this picture. Extend the end of the shuttle with a line at the top and two lines at the bottom. These will be **engine bays**.

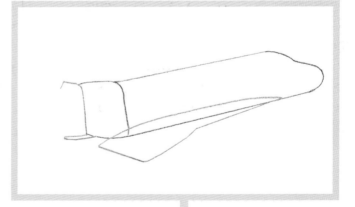

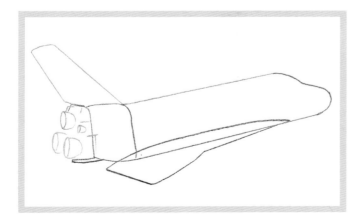

Step 3:

Draw three cup-shaped main engines on the end. Draw a smaller cup shape next to them for the control **thruster**. Add a triangle with the tip clipped off above the end. This is the tail.

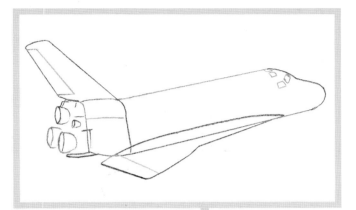

Step 4:

Use a straight line to divide the tail for a rudder. Draw **horizontal** lines on the ends. Then draw a line across the end of the wing for a wing flap. Add four small rectangular windows above the nose.

Step 5:

Draw a line along the tail and wing edge. Draw a line along the side of the shuttle. End the line behind the windows and make a sharp angle to the top. Use twelve dots to mark door hinges. Draw three short lines like a Z on the nose.

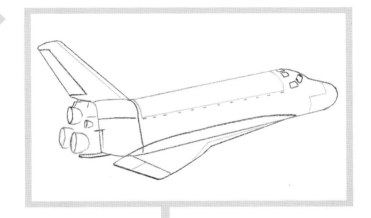

Step 6:

Shade the nose and the lines on the tail and wings. Shade the windows and the engine bay area. Write **NASA** on the wing and United States on the side. Add the American flag.

Space Station – Mir

The former Soviet Union launched the first **module** of the space station Mir in 1986. Over the years, Mir grew as modules were added. From 1986 to 2000, **astronauts** from many countries spent time on Mir collecting data and living in space. Mir was brought back down to Earth in March of 2001.

Step 1:

Draw a cylinder with one curved end and one oval end. Draw an oval to the left side. Draw another oval to the right side. These are the space station modules.

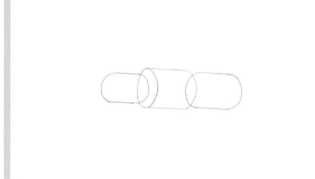

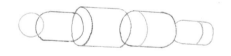

Step 2:

Add a circle to the left. Draw a curved line on the right oval. Then draw a bullet-shaped tube to the right. Draw a curved line across this shape.

Step 3:

Draw five different rectangles. Three go on the second module and two go on the end module. These are **solar panels**.

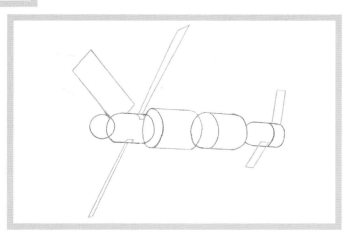

Step 4:

Draw two full circles and one partial circle on the first module. These are **docking ports**. Add small circles and curved and straight lines to the next two modules.

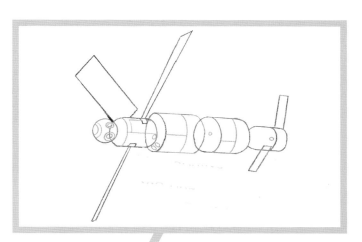

Step 5:

Divide the biggest solar panel in half lengthwise with two **parallel** lines. Draw short straight lines across the solar panels. Add a thick short line to the end of the first module.

Step 6:

Shade the docking ports. Add light shading to the rest of the body. Leave some white areas to show a gleam.

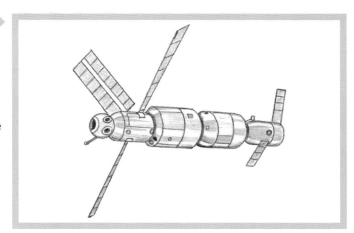

Titan IVB Rocket

The Titan family of rockets has been around since 1955, but this upgraded and more powerful Titan IVB first flew in 1997. It is an unmanned space booster used by the U.S. Air Force. Its job is to lift heavy satellites into space.

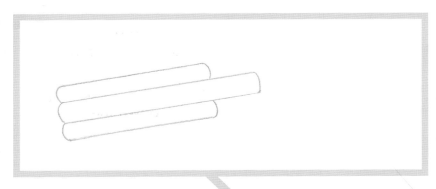

Step 1:
Draw three tubes next to each other. Make the middle tube longer than the two side tubes.

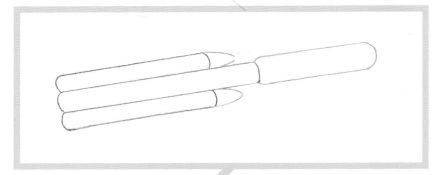

Step 2:
Draw half an oval on the end of each shorter tube. Add a large oval to the end of the middle tube.

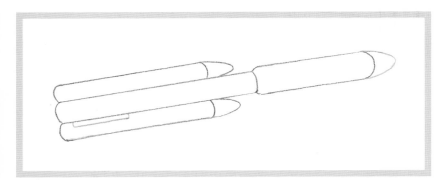

Step 3:
Add half of a pointed oval to make the nose cone on the middle tube. Draw half a rectangle on the bottom tube.

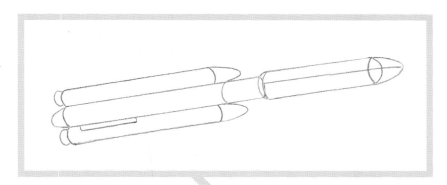

Step 4:

Draw C shapes at the left end of each tube. Add three curved lines, one across the tip of the nose and two near the center of the middle tube. Draw a line down the center of the forward tube to divide it in half.

Step 5:

Draw seven curved lines across each shorter tube. Draw five curved lines across the middle tube. Connect the tubes to each other with two thick lines near the tops of the shorter tubes. Draw two short **parallel** lines on the middle tube.

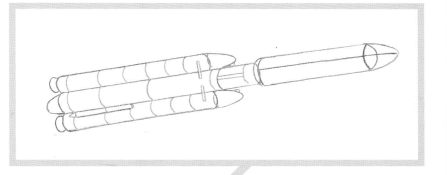

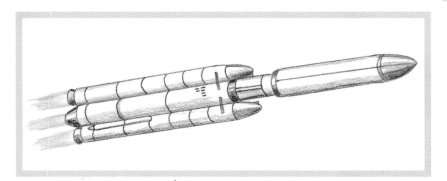

Step 6:

Shade all the rocket ends. Add three streams of rocket exhaust to make the Titan IVB look as if it is roaring through the **atmosphere**.

Mars Rover–Sojourner

When the Mars space **probe** landed in 1997, it set down the Mars rover named Sojourner. This six-wheeled rover collected information about Martian rocks, soil, and dust and sent the information back to scientists on Earth.

Step 1:

Draw a row of three circles. Draw a **horizontal** line above the circles. Draw short angled lines at each end of the line.

Step 2:

Draw half circles above each circle to make thick wheels. Draw small Cs for the wheel hubs. Connect each wheel to the bottom of the rover with short lines.

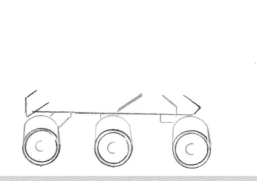

Step 3:

Draw a large rectangle above the wheels. Add two short **vertical** lines to the right side to connect it to the bottom of the rover.

Step 4:

Notch out the two corners on the left side of the rectangle by drawing two shapes that are like wide Vs. Draw four **parallel** lines across the rectangle. Then add short lines across each wheel.

Step 5:

Draw parallel lines across the rectangle to make a **crosshatch** pattern for the rover's **solar panel**. Use four short lines to draw the antenna on the upper left-side corner.

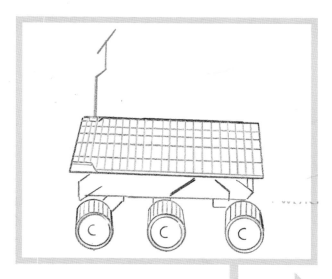

Step 6:

Shade the wheels and the bottom of the rover. Lightly shade the solar panel. Leave some white to show a gleam.

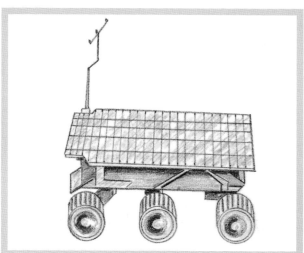

Intergalactic Fighter

The artist used his imagination to draw an imaginary high-speed space fighter. He calls it CimAdam MKI, or the Double Gull. You can copy this design or make your own imaginary fighter.

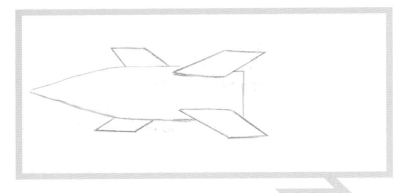

Step 1:

Draw a dart shape with one pointed end to make the body. Draw four diamond shapes, two on top and two below, to make four wings.

Step 2:

Add a thin, needle-like **horizontal** line to the edge of each wing.

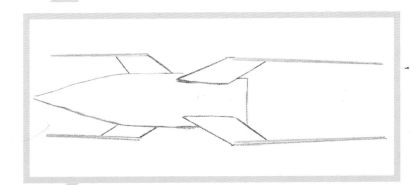

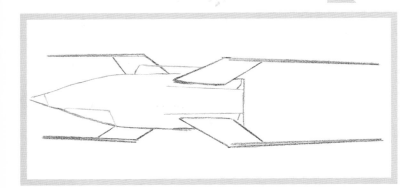

Step 3:

Draw a short line on the pointed nose and a half-rectangle shape on the side. Add a narrow rectangle to the top. Draw two **parallel** lines on the side between the two wings.

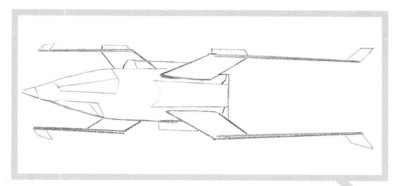

Step 4:

Draw diamond shapes at the ends of each needle line. Add a rectangle and a triangle on the nose for windows. Connect the two parallel lines on the body with a curve. Draw a half rectangle on the bottom of the fighter.

Step 5:

Draw a tiny rectangle on the nose and a triangle under the windows. Draw a line on the body just behind the **cockpit** windows. Add ovals to the top wings. Darken the short curved line on the body and make a small triangle at the top just behind the cockpit.

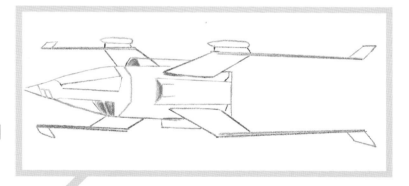

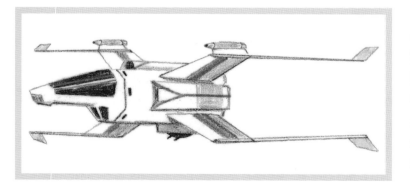

Step 6:

Darken the cockpit windows. Leave a thin line of white for the gleam in the glass. Add **shading** under the body of the fighter and your own markings.

Space Transporter

The artist calls his imaginary space transporter the FHF-3ST. It will carry heavy cargo over long distances in space. It will be the delivery truck of the stars. You can copy the design for this space transporter or design your own.

Step 1:

Start by drawing an umbrella shape. Give it a straight handle by drawing a shape like an ice-cream stick.

Step 2:

Add two more points to the points of the umbrella. Make the handle thicker by drawing a long tube with a circle at the top.

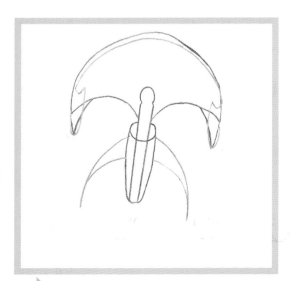

Step 3:

Draw a curved line above the top of the umbrella shape and round off the first points you drew. Add two curved wing shapes on either side of the handle. Make them end in sharp points.

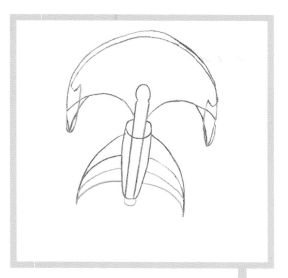

Step 4:
Draw a second set of pointed wings on either side of the handle. Add a tiny curve near the end of the handle.

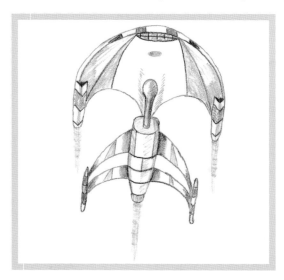

Step 5:
Draw thin ovals to connect the tips of the pointed wings. Add three more curved lines across the handle. Add two long curved lines to the umbrella shape. Connect them with one smaller curved line near the top. Make tiny curved lines at the tips of the top wings.

Step 6:
Add another curved line just in front of the top curve. Make two rectangles and two squares, and fill them in. Lightly **shade** the left and right sides of the curved wing, just above the side engines, to show depth. Add your own details, markings, and shading. Add rocket exhaust from the engines.

Planetary Explorer

Already, unmanned space **probes** visit distant planets and moons. But how will people explore space in the future? The artist has imagined this vehicle. He calls it the TGEV for **Terrestrial Geological** Exploration Vehicle.

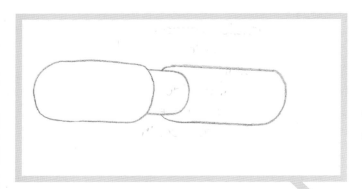

Step 1:

Draw two larger ovals next to each other. Connect them with half a smaller oval in the middle.

Step 2:

Add two curved bumps to the top and two short lines to the bottom. Attach half an oval on the end to the right. Draw a small oval shape underneath.

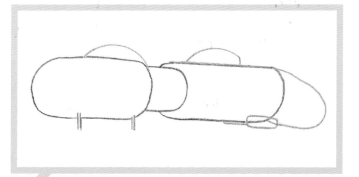

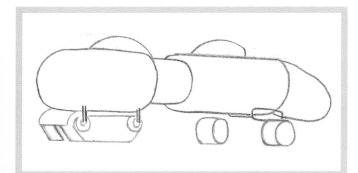

Step 3:

Add two tiny wheels to the ends of the two short lines. Draw a line around these two front wheels to make a belt. Draw three small rectangular shapes in front of these wheels. Then draw two larger wheels under the back end.

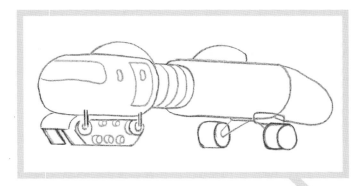

Step 4:

Add a big oval windshield and two small side windows. Draw a rectangle around one window for the door. Add little circles inside the belt for the wheels. Draw curved lines on the middle section and short, straight lines under the rear section to connect the wheels.

Step 5:

Add little oval headlights to the front. Draw a few **vertical** detail lines under the headlights. Draw short lines on the rectangles in the front. Divide the bumps on top with curved lines. Add curved lines and circles to the rear section. Add tread to the wheels and belts.

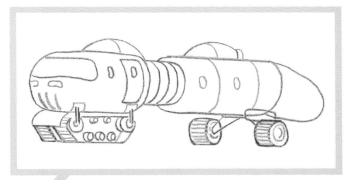

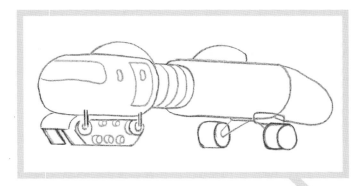

Step 6:

Add a pole-like crane to the side of the second bump on top. Darken the windows. Leave a little white in the windows to make it look like space-age glass. Add your own details and **shading.**

Space Station

Someday more people may live and work in space. The artist imagines that a future space station could look like this one. Like the old space station Mir, the **modules** of this station would be put together in space.

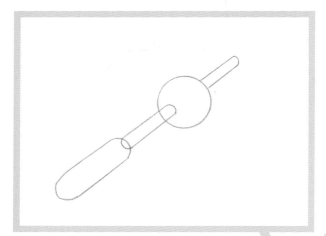

Step 1:

Draw a circle. Draw a narrow tube on either side. Then add a larger oval to the oval on the left. This makes four modules.

Step 2:

Add another oval to the tube on the right. This makes the fifth module. Add a small circle to the top of the round module. Add half an oval to the bottom of the round module and a tiny half rectangle to each side.

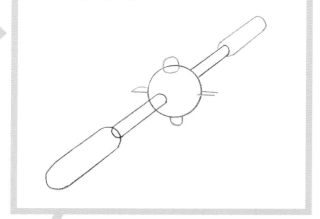

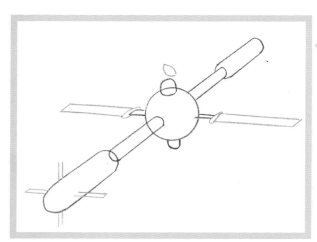

Step 3:

Draw a small oval and a long rectangle to each side of the round module to make **solar panels**. Add a small circle to the top of the space station. Use **parallel** lines to add four posts to the sides of the first module.

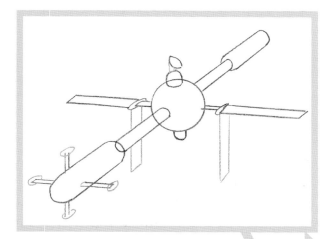

Step 4:

Add a small oval to the end of each post to make **docking ports** for other space vehicles. Add two more rectangular solar panels below the first two you drew. Use two tiny lines to connect the two small circles above the round module.

Step 5:

Add two curved lines across the round module. Draw a small arrow at the top of the smallest circle on top of the round module. Draw short lines across each end module. Fill in each of the four solar panels with short parallel lines.

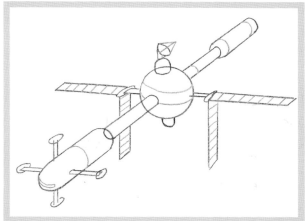

Step 6:

Add dots to the end modules to make windows. Add larger dark rectangular bands of windows to the round module. Draw a small curved line that connects the points of the arrow at the top of the space station. Add your own details and **shading**.

Glossary

astronaut crew member on a U.S. spacecraft

atmosphere gases, such as oxygen and nitrogen, that surround Earth

canopy sliding cover over the part of an aircraft where the pilot sits

capsule front section of a rocket that carries crew members and instruments into space

cockpit place where the pilot sits in an aircraft

docking port part of a space station to which visiting spacecraft can connect to unload people and equipment

doodling making little drawings at the edges of paper; cartooning

engine bay compartment on the spacecraft that holds the engine

fender frame over the wheel of a vehicle that protects the wheel and prevents splashing

geological having to do with the rock formations of an area

heat shield barrier that protects a space capsule as it comes in contact with the gases that surround Earth

lunar having to do with the moon

module self-contained unit, or part, of a larger system

NASA National Aeronautics and Space Administration, a United States agency that directs aerospace research

orbit path around a body in space; or to travel around a body in space

probe unmanned spacecraft that carries instruments to collect information

retrorocket small rocket at the front of a rocket or spacecraft that helps reduce speed when landing

solar panel device that collects heat from the sun in order to turn it into energy

stage section of a rocket that has its own engine and fuel

supersonic moving faster than the speed of sound

tailplane tail including the fins and rudder, which is used for steering aircraft

terrestrial having to do with land

test pilot pilot who flies new or experimental aircraft to check their performance

thruster exhaust that adds power to an aircraft's flight

Art Glossary

crosshatching
marking that uses lines that cross each other

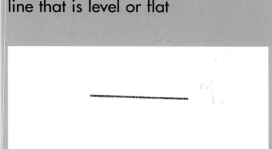

diagonal
line on an upward or downward slant

horizontal
line that is level or flat

kneaded eraser
soft, squeezable eraser used to soften dark pencil lines

parallel
straight lines that lie next to one another, but never touch

shade
make darker than the rest

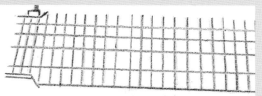

vertical
straight up and down

Find Out More

Books

Atkinson, Stuart. *Space Travel.* Chicago: Raintree, 2002.

Graham, Ian. *Space Vehicles.* Chicago: Raintree, 2006.

Visca, Curt, and Kelley Visca. *How to Draw Cartoon Spacecraft and Astronauts in Action.* New York: PowerKids Press, 2002.

Websites

NASA - Kids

http://kids.msfc.nasa.gov

Index